About the Author

Charlotte was born in England in 1970, is a graduate from Durham University, and an ex-sales director in IT from her corporate days. She is a mama and stepmama, and now finds herself somewhere between an entrepreneur and a witch. She shares her time between the Savoie mountains and the Provence vines in France, her chosen home for the last twenty-two years. She is a yoga and meditation teacher, life alignment coach, writer, and creative soul. Charlotte gets most of her inspiration from the naturescapes she lives in and writes from a uniquely intuitive place.

Resilience

Writings from the Heart to Inspire in Difficult Times

A Journey of Connection Back to You

Charlotte Saint Jean

Resilience

Writings from the Heart to Inspire in Difficult Times

A Journey of Connection Back to You

Vanguard Press

A CIP catalogue record for this title is
available from the British Library.

ISBN 978 1 80016 928 9

Vanguard Press is an imprint of
Pegasus Elliot Mackenzie Publishers Ltd.
www.pegasuspublishers.com

First Published in 2024

Vanguard Press
Sheraton House Castle Park
Cambridge England

Printed and Bound in Great Britain

Dedication

This book would not have been possible without the loving support of my partner, David. He has travelled with me to the depths — shared and our own — and together we have evolved along this beautiful path of anchoring, alignment, and abundance. Thank you for the cups of tea brought in silence with a smile and a kiss; thank you for listening to my madcap ideas and always keeping an open mind and a soft heart. Thank you to my daughters Mélodie and Clémentine, who continually inspire me as I stand in awe of our collective and individual creation. Thank you to my friend and photographer, Chris Harrison, for trekking up mountains to get the right photo. Thank you to the auspicious challenges in my life that have allowed me to accept, realign, and arise.

To Mélodie and Clémentine
My inspiration goddesses
Thank you

these are not tears
these are the sacred waters of my soul
inviting me to heal

Contents

A prayer to self.. 21

Simplicity Breath 24

Anchor... 26

Heart Notes 39

Acceptance 41

Heart Notes 53

Align... 55

Heart Notes 67

Abundance 69

Heart Notes 81

Arise 83

Heart Notes 95

Closing notes... 97

The Corporate Witch... 97

Finding my skin… This is my story...................... 99

When I was diagnosed with skin cancer my carefree kiss-the-sun lifestyle had to change swiftly. I did not want to give up the things I love, the connections with nature. This was not my time to hide away. Had I not found my calling? Had I not fought back from the depths of despair and once again found joy in the world, in life itself? Was I not a strong, positive, healthy woman? The news hit me hard. A cancerous melanoma. I went through all the characteristics of grief — disbelief, anger, deep sadness, fear, acceptance and then finally resilience.

This is not the first time I have faced the C word. In my early twenties an impersonal letter announced that treatment was necessary to remove what could emerge as ovarian cancer down the line. In my thirties the excruciating pain in my abdomen left me no option but to get help for intestinal cists. And now in my fifties with my Celtic skin and years of trying to be like my beautiful Mediterranean friends with their matt tones, my body sent out a message to respect and nourish myself differently.

As human beings we are resilient beyond measure — you may not feel this, but you are too. As women we are warriors of resilience. I have seen first-hand how the physical body heals, sometimes quickly, sometimes the path is longer. Our cells have a capacity to renew and the skin a wonderful talent to recreate itself. Just like the mycelium network beneath our feet, blood and tissue meanders through our body and creates miracles. From the ravages and beauty of childbirth to sports' accidents, from near death experiences to skin cancer, the body, I truly know, is a resilient beast. But this is just what you see on the outside — the one that grows, colours, fills out, drops down.

Resilience means fighting back in tough times, being the warrior, returning to battle where and when necessary. But resilient also means preparing the terrain, nourishing and nurturing physically, emotionally and energetically so that when challenges arise, we are ready and prepared to face it, them. We tend to err more on the outer layers, the ones that are seen, perceived. The internal energetic and emotional body, the one that integrates, adds layers of protection, the one that we don't see heal or hurt, often goes unnoticed. We ignore, forget, object, remember, get lost, find ourselves… All of this contributes to our inner and outer resilience. All of this enables the rich patchwork of who we are to shine brighter, stronger, better.

Resilience is a book that came to me after many lifetimes of experience, particularly in recent years, but not entirely. The whispers of childhood, of young adult life, the traumas and stories in finding my path, working through grief, toxic relationships, troubles, anger, deep sadness and abundant joy. The feelings of being totally alone, the depths of depression hidden from the outside world. The knowing who I am deep down and the inability to express that in 'acceptable' ways. This is a book that took form when I was diagnosed with skin cancer. I had already experienced traumas in the past, nearly dying when my second daughter came into this world, a near-fatal ski accident when a parallel moment in time fleetingly washed over me. I have seen angels and trusted in my own physical capacity to patch back my body. I have faced the entrails left behind after suicide, the pain when your children are hurting so much and you can't quite reach them.

I know the body is resilient — I have watched it heal and recreate itself, literally. Just like bowls that have their cracks repaired using the Japanese method of Kintsugi, honouring their cracks and being put back together to make a stronger, more beautiful bowl, I have watched as the scar on my leg offers proof of this resilient beauty. However, the mind is also an extremely powerful, sometimes stubborn, and resilient messenger itself, carrying energy and meaning in its words and detailed inner conversations.

This book also emerged at a time when my own body was going through the transition of the menopause, a very real, physical rite of passage that each woman faces with very different experiences, apprehensions and emotions. It is a time of life often ignored by those around you. It is as if it doesn't exist if we don't talk about it, integrate it. And yet it does happen, affects all women and is a very real experience that emotionally, physically, mentally, and I would add spiritually, changes us.

The Asian traditions call this time the 'second spring' and despite social stigma, I would agree. There is a sort of grey wash that the vibrant youthful world wishes to paint over this time. Many women feel ignored, unseen. So much so that I see many women dye their hair and cut it short, wear huge colourful jewellery and paint their faces back on at that this time in their life in a vain hope to be seen again, but many more who drift into the beige, grey and unremarkable blues of the latter middle-ages and beyond. We dye, hide, mask, create and try to be seen (or not) whilst mourning what was, what is past. This book is therefore a reclaiming of life in the second spring of it, a celebration of the wisdom goddess if you will. This is a time to revel in the freedom that this wonderful period of our human form allows us.

This book represents musings not for the mind to analyse but the body and soul to feel, to peel away the layers, to let the barriers go and to let yourself dive into the feeling body — this is how you feed the alleyways and pathways of otherness. This allows you to feel with your mind and think with your heart, offering you some guidance towards your own connections, to your source, to your Dharma.[1] *Resilience* is a collection of texts and poetry to inspire, to provide solace and serenity, to provide grounding when needed. It is a book you go to when you are feeling misaligned, derailed and a little lower than normal but also one that can simply encourage more joy, love and abundance. The words can act as a massive hug, a reminder that you are not alone, that others have walked this path too.

---

[1] Dharma is your life's mission, your sacred contract on this earth plane

Words are so important to me. I collect them. I speak four languages and five if you count the one that is somewhere between English and the divine, slightly Arabic, guttural, visceral noises that take their source from distant lands and far off seas. Words are vital to our creative inspiration. They encourage feelings, emotions, the undercurrents of existence. In Japanese there are many words that describe sounds, experiences. One special word, Yügen, has a beautiful meaning: 'the indescribable, that which cannot be told in words'. Although this is a collection of texts, of poetry and words, some things cannot be explained in a few letters that 'collect together' and are read out. There are hidden pathways and meanings that are perceived or rather felt by the reader that day, that season, that time in their life path.

The book that you hold in your hands is an offering from my heart to yours. It is divided into five sections; Anchor, Acceptance, Align, Abundance, Arise, each of these chapters created from what I feel are the rights of passage from the depths of grief to the heights of joy. We need to anchor and find our own roots, our own source before we can really do anything else. We need to truly feel this. We should accept and allow the soft animal of who we really are before moving forwards to manifest newness. We can open then to alignment, integrating who we are with the accepted pathway for growth. Then we can open the doors to abundance and invite joyful movement, freedom, into our arising.

All are vital ingredients for being fully ourselves.

I have chosen A words for the chapters as this is the first letter of the English alphabet and the first letter of the family name I was christened with, Allen. This is to honour my family who I love deeply but I think have never truly understood where I came from and who I am but accept me anyway. There are fifty-two texts or poems as I turned fifty-two when this book was written. There are fifty-two weeks in the year and five decades that I have been on this beautiful planet in this sacred form. It is my hope, wish, desire that these words can also whisper to your soul and help you smile quietly to yourself as you read them sitting exactly where you are, in the here and now. All have come from whispered moments and ancestral guidance, from inner sovereignty and soft, subtle empowerment. May you live like the lotus flower, firmly rooted in the mud of life, shining brightly through petals of love and honour your true message.

In love and light, from heart to yours. Namaste.[2]

---

[2] Namaste means the divine sweetness in me salutes the divine sweetness in you.

A Prayer to Self
For Times When I forget Who I am

I am she

I was the girl who galloped through the forests
who ran through bluebell woods
who listened to the whisper of the wind
who danced freely in the rain

I was the girl who prayed alone each night in her darkened
    room
who came alive at Sunday worship
who lay in wheatfields and watched the clouds
who nuzzled into her horse's care

I am the woman who runs with the wolves
who sings to the trees
who bathes in wild waters and forests
who flies with no wings and howls at the full moon

I am the woman who climbs mountains and steps lightly
    on the earth
who kisses the sky and soars with the eagles
who watches the robin feed and the heron glide
who lives in mountain meadows and dances under the stars

I am the woman who lets her angels guide her
I am that girl
I am that woman
I am SHE

Simplicity Breath

Anchor down, tune in

Before you read this book, just a few words of guidance.
You can either read the book in the classic way, from
start to finish or choose to dip in and out as needed.
You can take notes, scribble on the pages, add your
own sticky notes...

But before you do, before you allow the soft whispers of
your soul to wrap you in warm cotton...

Sit down on the earth, just for a while
Just for a few breaths and come into the now, into the
feeling body

Take a few moments of time out, just for you

As you inhale anchor down into your roots
BE

As you exhale, tune in to what matters to
YOU

What is the energetic architecture you wish to create

Breathe here a while

Until things seem calmer
Until you feel you are

PRESENT

Stay a while in silent contemplation

Now… Read on

Anchor

when attached, weighted down, moored to the seabed to
stop you drifting
a symbol of salvation and a steady belief or hope to offer
safety and security

and so I sit
I feel the earth
I let the roots embroider their way into my body
I breathe deeply into the present
I root down
drop anchor
fall into her arms
I am

I call upon

I call upon all those here present
listening between sky and earth
to bring forward light and love
to offer space to my tired body
to breathe into my heart

I call upon the healing light of my angels
may they protect and guide me
along this path
to feel at home

I call upon this moment
in time to tune into
my inner voice
to feel the soft vibration
of my heart

Let me fly without wings
Walk without feet
Sing without words

Let me be simply me

I can fall no further… hope in dark times

I can fall no further
than the earth, than the soft wet grass
and the smell of damp leaves

I can fall no further
than the rocks and rubble
than this gravel pit of empty emotion

I can fall no further
than the riverbed
and the soft folds of the stream

I can fall no further
than this sacred ground
that softens and heals

I can fall no further

but I can watch the clouds drift by
as the whisper of the wind brushes the skin
with the promise of hope

I can feel the heart soften
my roots thicken
my connection deepens

and as I breathe gently into the trunk of the universe
I can rise into my own truth

I am not enough

I am not enough
an eternal mantra
hunting, haunting me
pushing me to collide
with ever-increasing
circles of activity and newness

I am not quite there, just a little more
but if I do this, it will be okay
the lights will go on
and the trumpets sound, for I have made it

I am not enough
but I know if I push myself
just that bit further, I will get there
the warrior in me will guide me, won't she?

I am... me, not enough
not quite there, a weary warrior
but perfectly imperfect trying so hard to be
what I have always been... myself
and then she whispers
be kinder to yourself, sister, let go
you are a human body in an ancient soul
and you are perfectly
just as you were meant to be

stronger than a rose

she stands tall, firm, strong
attached and rooted
to a source of life
only she knows

she protects from those
who wish to take her
arms at the ready
to quietly fight back

she shines, radiates and
fans out her beauty
opening gently the many
layers of who, what and why

colour vibrating for all to see
she kept her secrets
cloaked in robes and worlds of rainbows
she is stronger than a rose

bowing to sovereignty

take a breath
breathe deeply
draw the air inwards
then let if fall down
caressing the inner rivers
until it lands lightly
on sacred soil

here, breathe again
a breath only you know
one that journeys with you
too far off lands you call
home

then stay here a while
rest in the inner knowing
breathe even deeper
allow the quiet whisper
of your kingdom to nourish you

bow softly to sovereignty

the white wolf

can you see her?
the old white wolf
wise at my side as she gently guides me
in the 'right' direction

can you hear her?
as she nuzzles into me
and I lean into her
ragged and nourishing coat

can you feel her?
no words needed
just the gentle knowing
the perfect protection
she is there
kind, secret, deeply, comforting

the white wolf
never leaves my side

tememos

there is a landscape
that travels with you
a delicate border
that protects
quilts you in a loving protection
and holds you
when the tears flow

there is an energy
that shelters you
that reaches up and out
to nurture you
cloaks you in kindness and
encourages you
to move forwards into joy
to reach your arms to the sky
and sing

and on a day like any other

and on a day like any other
she spent time to reconnect
she reassessed and evolved
she stood firm and grounded
she marvelled at the beauty around her
she took a deep breath
she let herself
drift into the inner knowing

on a day like any other
she realised
she knew she belonged
she was exactly who she had always
dreamed she could be

trust

trust
walk quietly, one step at a time
each one a gentle reminded
that you can

believe
as you move through the world
believe you are all that
you ever imagined you
could be

breathe
then breathe deeply into the
inner knowing
that ancient river in you
you have all the answers
right there, waiting

Trust
Believe
Breathe

devotion

lying on the forest floor
small purple flowers and pinecones for company
I believe deeply
devotion comes from rich moments
that smell of leaves and kaleidoscopes of
connection

commitment comes from showing up
believing you can, that all is possible
loving comes from time spent in silence
and in the roar of passion

as the branches move and the wind
whispers, I let my heart soften
my mind rises, my body descends
I tune into the deepest resources of my soul
and I let the forest's promise
guide me home

Heart Notes

_____
_____
_____
_____
_____
_____
_____
_____
_____
_____
_____
_____
_____
_____
_____
_____
_____
_____
_____
_____
_____
_____
_____
_____
_____
_____
_____
_____
_____

Acceptance

When you believe something to be true, valid, correct and are willing to receive this truth willingly, to approve the state you are in or the new state you are welcoming.

and so I breathe and let go
this is my time
this is the moment
to simply… BE
to consent to what is
to receive what is mine
to recognise that these are precious gifts
to approve and accept them all
I am open to it all
I feel
I am

sit in silence

I am alone, my back against the willow trunk
the waters flowing by

this time it feels right
to sit awhile in silence
the solitude warm and nourishing
like a blanket of love

I am alone
but the willow's whispers
move my soul and sing to my heart
the ancient cathedral stones
nourish my thoughts
and flow through
me like the waters running at my side

the silence is palpable
the deep rich tones echo beneath
the stones, the roots, the earth,
reminding me of past lives and dreams
tracing lines with ancestral heritage

so I sit with her,
in the soft silence and breathe

can you hear me?

I am listening, can you hear me?
from deep within
from a long time back
when ancient songs formed in my mouth
in my heart, in my soul

I am listening, can you hear me?
from far off lands
of the beating drum and the horn
from the galloping stallion and the bow
flung over my fur clad shoulder

I am listening, can you hear me?
from the babbling brook and the eagle's wing
from the great bark of the forest guardians
from the whisper of the wind

Can you hear me?
because
I
am
listening…

feel to heal

but it hurts
it pulls at me and darkens my inner kingdom
it drags me under the waves
it calls out to me

but it hurts
so I will lie for a while
here on the earth
I will let her roots
her grounded, musty smell
seep into my body
but it hurts
so I will cry for a while
let the salty, sacred waters cleanse me
clean the dark corridors
I have been too strong for too long

but it hurts
and yet the more I feel
the more I let the twisted branches
ruffle my feathers
the wild winds guide me
the more
I heal

let your breath breathe you

let your breath, your own perfect, soft breath
breathe you

just for a moment
let the quiet whisper within
be the queen of this huge inner empire

let the swirl of air
flying over the treetops
rejuvenate your soul
illuminate the darkest corners

let your breath breathe you
devour your inhale
worship your exhale

let the quiet empress
flow
freely

sit with your own transparency
let your breath
breathe you

rain drops whisper

it's quiet, almost not there
but if you lean into the
soft arc of the wind
if you let the rain guide you
you can hear the drops whisper

they don't shout out loud
or stamp and scream
they don't force or push
they quietly fall
and whisper to the innermost
alleys of your soul

raindrops whisper
they tell secrets
they sing quietly
they fall peacefully
and keep you wrapped in softness

resilience

just another word
used often, wrongly
resilient, warrior like we fight back
we are strong, cold, able bodies

yet resilience comes in colours, flavours
streams through your every vein
arms you with strength, power, intuition
a safety net to protect
an army to attack

she is the warrior goddess of preparation

she is the wild woman of wisdom

she transforms, protects, nourishes

resilience

not just another word
I am
She

She is
You

from now on

from now on
I will stand in my own strength
I will fight my own battles
I will own who I am

from now on I will soften
when I need to
I will show myself love and empathy
I will live freely

from now on
I will listen to my intuition
I will let the whisper guide my path
I will speak my truth

from now on
I will nourish the wild woman
I will harness her power
I will use her wisdom

from now on
I will be the essence
I am here to be
I will embody
all my qualities
all my strengths all my weaknesses
from now on I will be me

mother earth, sister river

mother earth, sister river
grandmother forest
guide my steps
to tread the path my ancestors took

take my hand and lead me
down paths and riverbeds
beyond the waterfalls and haze
nudge me gently closer
to the source of
all light

mother earth, sister river
grandmother forest
guide my voice to sing
beauty and truth
as the dawn raises its head
and bows low
let me merge with you
for you know the way

I receive

should I consent to this?
will it go away if I ignore it?
if I approve of this, will it make it right, better?

I sit alone in the bathroom, wondering where it has all gone
the tight skin, the tautness, time past
the sun and age spots trace a life lived fully
the sag here and there, the passage of the years
the wrinkles around the mouth, the corner of the eyes...
all mapping out the reality that I am living
I have stopped bleeding
I realise I can't remember the last time I did
I feel sadness creep over me, again
belief, recognition, something that is offered, gifted to me
but I didn't order this, did I?

maybe I did, maybe I should
if I receive this time as a wisdom gift
as the whisper of the winds promises
if I consent to this passage and honour it
if I recognise that incredibleness of what I can do,
not still do but the new things I am able to achieve
then I will open the shutters to my second spring
no need to pale things out
no need to paint things on
I can accept, receive and be
the most incredible me

closure

so I sorted the box
and arranged the contents
I spread everything on the floor
and looked for a long while
at the parts of my life
that no longer serve me

patchworks and fragments of living
moments and snippets that represent
months and years of time
colourful shards that serve as reminder
of good and bad times

am I that piece of clothing?
that book, necklace, ring, scarf?

where am I in the maze of memorabilia
not in these things
not in these objects
but here in this heart,
this moment
this breath,
this smile

Heart Notes

Align

When I line everything up, arrange things in order to help, to lift up, to support

and so I take a step
I notice how I place my feet
how my words leave my heart
how I arrange my body
I take stock
I reassess
I seek harmony in the chaos
I allow the gentle waters
of transformation to flow
I act
I am

the tribe

You do not walk alone, she said
you stand in a long line of warrior
women, sure strength at their core

You run with the white wolf and the black bird
you are guided back by the falcon,
the owl's cry, the spider's web
you gallop with the black horse
and fly high with the eagle

You do not walk alone, she said
you step lightly with the deer,
you hop with the frogs
and flutter with the butterfly

You do not walk alone, she said
you stride forwards with the white bear
right by your side

You do not walk alone, she said
you walk united with your tribe

find that, which was never lost

it was never lost
it never went away
you just forgot a while

it is there within you
it never leaves your side
it breathes in your bones
it whispers to every cell
it envelopes you in its love

it is you

find that,
which was never lost
and hold it tight

seek the food that nourishes your soul

Gone is the time of the lone wolf
it is time to fling open the doors
welcome the strangers in
nourish the soul by allowing others
to belong to you

Gone is the time of single focussed living
it is time to soften our hearts
keep a strong back
a keen eye and a curious mind

it is time to belong to you

Gone is the time for progress
it is time to create communities
lean into the soft wisdom inside that just is
the knowing of generations past
it is time to belong
again

resist and flow

it pushes and pulls you along
you follow at first but then there is resistance
something pulling you down
pushing you back

you stand at the cliff edge
looking out into the unknown
feeling the crashing weight of what might be
wanting to break free and be alone

then you let yourself go
you dive into the cool pools of
promise
of the mystery below
you let the waters bring you back to life
nourish your skin
enliven your soul

you resist no more
you let the ebb and flow glisten,
glide and gently press you
forwards

follow the light

you know where you are going
you listen
you tune into your soul
and she guides you, calls you

your ancestors trod this earth
now you walk this path
the light
it shines way beyond your door

just follow the light, she says
you may not know why
or where you came from
but you know she will guide you
home, or forwards, or away
in love

you may not know where you are going
but you know
she will guide you
home, forwards, in love

and above all in truth

speak from behind your eyes

don't block it out
shroud your truth
pretend to paint the cracks away

don't let the bright colours
blind you
dive deeply into the purple pods of honesty

don't stop the flowing
as the whirlpools of reality
cloud over your vision

dive in deep
speak from behind your eyes
you will always walk the right path

Clumsy Clara's world of light

Step lightly
remember the little people
live in the blades of grass
hide under the mushrooms

Step lightly
remember your steps kiss the earth
with footprints so light,
so gentle that you pass almost unnoticed,
except you don't

Step lightly into the world of dreams
of magical rainbows and gold-filled pots
where you dance and glide like an angel's wing
like the ballet dancer you dreamt of being
not the watering can fairy
they made you dress-up as

Step lightly, my child, full of grace
in between the rocks and glades
over stone and stream into the promised land
of wild, connected freedom

tears the sacred gateway

don't cry, she said
it will all be okay
as she gently wiped away my tears
and the blood from my grazed knees
she reached for the biscuit jar
the smell of butter, warmth and love
wrapped me in a blanket of care

don't cry, she said, it will all be okay
as she gently wiped my back, my arms, my hands
let the tears drop gently down my face
no words needed
she reached for the chart on the end of the bed
smiled and wrote something unknown to me
perfectly describing the emptiness I felt
the beeps, the pump that endlessly
worked its life magic,
no biscuit jar,
no buttery hugs

so I closed my eyes
allowed the tears to flow
roll onto my body
cleansing the strong barriers
that had been there for too long
opening sacred gateways
to evolve, to grow, to soften.

waterfall grace

when did you hear her calling to your soul?
was it when the waters crashed down
into the pool of dark mystery?
was it when you let your body
touch the icy lair of her depths?
or was it when you drifted,
naked as a child
across the mirrored surface

no matter
you knew
she was there to wash away your pain
to cleanse the suffering
she was there to heal you
to wrap you in her watery cavern
tell you it will be okay

there will be a time of laughter
and dance again
but for now
lay here a while
before you swim to the shore

when I tune in

when I tune in
to the whisper of the trees
I can find infinite truths

when I listen to the leaves
sing I can find balance
in me

when I capture
the song of the swallows
as they fly
soaring high above
I can find freedom
here on earth

when I let go
of the past
I can walk calmly
into the truth
of my future

Heart Notes

Abundance

When a large quantity, an ample amount of whatever you
need lands lightly in your lap

and so I welcome abundance
I open my heart wide
I allow the rich tapestry of life to wrap itself around me
I breathe deeply and slowly
then I open my arms wide
smile
and allow the sweet moment of now
to embrace the world
I love

seasons shift

there is a time
of fresh water and new leaves
when droplets of dew offer
bathing pools for the smallest goddesses
to cleanse in

there is a time
of harsh clouds
of gusty winds
when the wild child of youth
takes the reins and
flies not a care in the world
there is a time
of morning mists
of chilly air
when you feel alive
when nothing else matters

there is a time
of fiery colours
of auburn tones
of wood fires and smoke signals
of whispering leaves and mystery
there is a time of expectation
when the buzzard flies
before the snows arrive and place a blanket
of love on the world

where does your love flow

as I sit here between sun and earth
I allow a soft whisper of wind
to gather me up
to guide me home
I breathe deeply into my soul
I open to the tiniest possibility of love
I allow the earth to support me
I allow the waters to flow through me
I allow the air to open the closed corners of my heart
I allow the space to course through my veins
I let go
I release control

then
as I sit
it comes to me
if today is the day I lose it all
give me enough strength to forget,
to forgive,
to let it be

give me enough strength
to love myself
to lift my head and be
me

opening the shutters of time

the mist rises in between the forest scape
the mountains frame the dawning sun
there is a light breeze flowing
through the crack in the window
gently telling me to trust

look up, cry the swallows
as they dive and swoop
don't get down
don't give up
join our dance
come fly amongst the clouds
sing your own song

a distant dog calls out
the cat purrs around my legs
impatient to meditate
in the soft folds of my lap

and so I sit a while
and breathe
and watch the whisper of the windchime sound
its wakeup call and I know
it is time
to open the shutters

the robin's song

she comes softly
hopping lightly with joy
and stares at the window
she has been away for some time now
but faithfully,
patiently returns
when the time is right
when I need her most of all

I wait for her
I know she will come
she knows I will wait
I always do

a touch of joy
a sprinkle of wisdom
a hop and skip of love
of lightness
of hope
but most of all
trust

she knows
and somehow
so do I

keep a strong back and an open heart

Keep a strong back and an open heart
she said in soft tones
across the network
from a far off living room
that spoke quietly deep within me

Keep a strong back and an open heart
because you can
because you want to
this is your path forwards
spine strong,
confident in its verticality
heart open
soft, gentle
because whatever else goes on
your heart will lead you
to the valley of love

keep a strong back and an open heart, she whispered
as if a distant memory
was guiding me
whispering to my spirit
she knows there are days when the wildflowers dance
and the body sings in multicolour
tracing rainbows across the grass
and those days can be lived
at any moment if you let them

we are spirit children

guardians of the forest
grandmothers of guidance
let our steps be light
let our hearts be open
allow our inner rhythm
to nudge us gently
where we know
we need to journey

guardians of the forest
grandmother souls
sing to us softly
a lullaby of peace
gently wrap us in your cloak of light
fill our hearts with love

guardians of the forest
warriors of mystery
speak to us in wild languages
let us understand
each sound as a truth
as a song of wisdom
as a beacon guiding us home

the enchanted tree

the hills roll past in sweeping gestures
the familiar train
gliding through
horse and wheat clad pastures
the grey and orange stone houses
whoosh past
with the promises of warmth and love
the sad song of disappointment
all too close

I cloud watch
catching dreams and whispers
in the air
as the world dashes past
forgotten notes of apology
drift behind me

and then there she is
the enchanted tree
large trunk
comforting arms
treasured isles
mystical creatures
laughter and invention
filter down I lean back
into her familiar strength
I am home and home is in me

the back step

it is sunday morning
I am sitting on the back step
the early morning sun streaming down
the radio chatting away
with my parents
in the kitchen
I am shelling peas

beside me is a red book
the history of ballet
holding promises and images
I know don't belong to me
but the graceful gaze
of otherness
attracts me

my chubby legs
hold a bowl of green circles
perfect in their fresh newness
the husks lay on the floor
waiting to be filled
or rejected
and all is well with the world
I am five years old and yet
I am hundreds more

the selkie skin

"where did you last leave it?"
comes the cry from downstairs
it knocks
me sideways
so I sit on the top step
hold my breath

she is talking about a coat
the one she bought for me
the one I have worn for years
the one that is now too small for me,
tight, ill-fitting
and yet still she insists I wear it

"so where did you last leave it?"
I start to breathe again
I have no idea where it is
but I know now is the time
to lose it
for good
find a new one
one that fits me
one that I choose
that is all my own creation
and that makes me dance
carefree
in the light of the full moon

it is time

suddenly, in the middle of the night
I am awake
alert
there is a fuzzy, intense sensation
buzzing around my head
beating in my heart
troubling my tummy
where am I?

the two a.m. heat flush
the full moon's glare
the late night message from my daughter
(is she home okay?)
the bathroom dash
the sip of water
take a breath
the now familiar midnight call
it is time

a drop of oil
a sip of water
a glance at the moon
a deep breath
and I snuggle down for a few more hours
tomorrow I will tackle this accept that it is time
I am fine with this
my time has come to be fully woman it is time

Heart Notes

Arise

When things just make sense, become real, apparent, emerge from nowhere, she will arise

and so I stand tall
I emerge from the darkness
I allow myself to shine
to let the light within
guide me
to shimmer in the depths
and fly high above the treetops
I arise like a new morning dawn
I see, I serve, I rise
I am

the forest mists

can you see me swirl and twist
can you see me speak
to your spirit
when the early morning
lifts the curtains
welcomes the dawn
can you see it spiral around
into your truth?

can you feel me swirl and twist
can you feel me speak to your soul
when the moon wanes and sings
to your heart
can you feel it spiral around
into who you are?

can you sense me swirl and twist
can you sense me speak to your soul
when the subtle mists flow
the light is soft
can you sense me spiral
inside you too?

and the forest mists
herald a new dawn
a new age
a new you

she

she looked for many years
to find who she was

she walked the mountain paths
she climbed high
she swam rivers
she dived into deep waters
she walked through fires
she stayed alone
silent in deep
pools of thought
she flew with the clouds
she followed the moon
she danced with the stars

she looked for many years to
find who she was

when all along
she had always been
who she dreamed
she could be

have the courage to dance in the flames

take my hand
you know you can
it is time
take a deep breath
walk with me into the shadows
towards the light it will be okay trust me

do you feel the heat
let go walk through
to the other side
let the light inside
guide you

now dance, goddess
in the flames
in the love
in joy
in the pool of light
that is you

the eagle's flight

the snows are coming
they ride in the crisp November air
dance naked
on the rust-coloured grass
there is a promise
gliding on the trees
a magical moment
just waiting to land

the snows are coming
they run across the sky
inviting your wild soul to sing
and follow
there is a crisp edge to the air
as I sit and wait
for their white coats to descend
but just before it does
the skies darken
there is a faint whisper
a swoop a flight of freedom
as the eagle
majestically calls out
and rides on an invisible tide
of hope

walk the path, fly the kite

don't be frightened, she said
your light will illuminate
the path
you will know where to tread
which way to go

how, she replied,
there are no signs!
trust in yourself
breathe deeply and tune in
your spirit light will guide you

so she sat still
took a deep breath
and listened
above her head
a kite flew
dancing in the song of the wind

and she knew
she was free

rainbows and unicorns

there is a pot of gold
at the end of the rainbow
they say
but how do you find the end?

will the purples
promising mystery take you?
the lush green ride and guide you?
the fiery reds and yellows burn shafts of light in you?
will the blue's nurturing gaze
lead you?
the orange set in the sun
open a gateway?

but no matter how much we tell ourselves
it's not true
it can't be
we want to believe
we know it 'could' be
and we know that to get there
we will ride proud
on a glorious
unicorn

dragonfly's wings

just for a few days the colours fly free
darting blues and vibrant greens
seeking communion,
community
flights of beauty
of passion
of desire

flitting here and there
dancing in the air
with life, love
just for a few days
the colours fly free
joining the dots
they pull you in
encourage

but
beware
the moment you try to intervene
share their beauty
capture the moment
just for you
they are gone free far away
no constraint
follow their lead

making rainbows, creating spirals

our stories have lives of their own
and it is up to us
to make them mean
something

each one a captured moment
a whisper
a fleeting shaft
of colour
of light
of dreams

each chapter
a new beginning
a welcome opening
to newness
to invention
to possibility
each story matters
even those shrugged off
in boredom, anger
on a wet Monday morning
especially those that
have never quite finished
your stories have lives
of their own, and it is up to you
to make yours count

full moon promise

shining benevolence
breathing life hop
grandmother moon
remind us

remind the mothers
that they are loved
brave
magnificent

remind the sisters
that they are strong
resilient
forgiving

remind the daughters
that they are worthy
beautiful
powerful

let the circle of women
go on

let your light
guide us

mountain paths, true summits

she guided me up and up
through the deep mystery of the forest
where the damp coolness
sent shivers over me
but I walked on
she guided me up and up
along shale paths
and hard packed tracks
along grassy tufts and blueberry bushes
but I walked on

she guided me up and up
higher than I have ever been
higher than I thought I could go
the air was thinner
the sun hotter
but I walked on
she guided me there
to the summit
the very ceiling of the world
and I stopped, looked down
way down below
I felt smaller than ever before
and yet stronger
brighter, truer
and I knew that I could, that I can that I belong

Heart Notes

_____
_____
_____
_____
_____
_____
_____
_____
_____
_____
_____
_____
_____
_____
_____
_____
_____
_____
_____
_____
_____
_____
_____
_____
_____
_____

Closing notes

The Corporate Witch

A while ago, I was asked to describe what I do and after failing to truly get across the intuitive spirit that guides me for each offering I dived in and said, "I am somewhere between corporate and witch."

This pretty much sums me up. Or as the Bhagavad Gita says, 'Keep one hand in society but the heart in the divine'. I have tried to maintain a stable and practical base for my life whilst always tuning in to the wild woman wisdom within, that soft voice that whispers through the forest branches and mountain waterfalls. I have nourished my family with a happy, safe home, food on the table but the knowledge that we are free at any time to go and dance in the rain, howl at the moon or lie on the earth just because.

As a young girl, I hid my 'difference', nurturing quietly in the night the fact that I didn't quite get the outside world and took solace in the church, in the quiet musty smell, the old stones and the cold wooden benches. I revelled in the evensong and the quiet moments of prayer. As much as I tried to keep this a secret, to even ignore its pull, the spirit pulled hard. I travelled through classic pathways, tried hard to 'succeed' in the 'real world' of commerce and yes, I learnt skills, added to the colourful patchwork of my talents; but something else yearned inside me. It ate away inside me and no matter how I tried to control its desire, to stifle the pain I was feeling in the outside world, it did not give up on me. Until one day, lying in a hospital bed, I felt a shift, a pull, not an urgent one, but a portal that opened and gently encouraged me to leave that world behind.

Several hospital beds, some angel meetings and two children later I realised, finally, I could be me. I could use the skills from the past, the dull ache within me, to be positive, joyful and live in the outside world as I did inside. I could walk with the wolf, gallop through the meadows and follow the tracks in the forest and still pay my taxes and nurture my family. I truly hope from the bottom of my heart that these words touch your soul, your spirit. Close your eyes and breathe deeply. The journey is just beginning.

Finding My Skin... This Is My Story

In ancient lands they tell stories of shapeshifting women and of the Selkie tribe, seal women who shed their skin to dance in the light of the moon and then put them back on to swim off into the deep seas. They tell of a Selkie whose skin gets stolen and despite her trying to fit into her new skin she never could and she lost her colour, her sparkle and her zest for life. My creative story started at a time when I had lost myself, my skin, in a world of stress, success, expectation and city living. Yoga found me at this time and after a great number of years, failings and micro successes, I learnt to lean into my intuitive voices and find me. Channelling this divine light became my path of service. I hope to share some of that with you in the mountains, cities, in the pages of this book, wherever life chooses to take us.

One very hot summer in the heart of the Ardèche, I watched as hundreds of dragonflies danced on the waters of the river. Attracted by their vibrant blue beauty, I wanted to get one for myself, with no force, just to see a little closer. After a few magical moments of connection several landed on my arm, and wanting to get an even closer look, I tried to hold onto one... and that is when she tipped her tail and bit me. And that, my friends, is me — free, never put me in cage, never place me in a category otherwise I may bite.

As she steps out onto the pebbled beach
and the waters lap over her toes
she knows

Deep within the quiet whispers
of the wild gently watch over her
she walks with gentle steps
and lets the water get higher up
her shivering thighs

Magic waters and bright blue skies
a moment's hesitation
a cry from a distant eagle
the perfume of a summer flower
and the light jump of a mountain trout
she knows

And so, the waters guide her further
she lets her body go into the
freezing lake
the wild woman singing alongside her
and the quiet wolf howling silently
watching from the shore
she knows